PIANO • VOCAL • GUITAR

BEST OF
RASCAL FLATTS

ISBN 978-1-4950-9446-0

HAL•LEONARD®
7777 W. BLUEMOUND RD. P.O. BOX 13819 MILWAUKEE, WI 53213

Visit Hal Leonard Online at
www.halleonard.com

BLESS THE BROKEN ROAD

Words and Music by MARCUS HUMMON,
BOBBY BOYD and JEFF HANNA

FAST CARS AND FREEDOM

Words and Music by GARY LEVOX,
WENDELL MOBLEY and NEIL THRASHER

* Recorded a half step higher.

I see a dust _____ trail fol-low-in' an old _____ red No-va, ba-

by blue eyes, _____ your head _____ on my shoul - der. _____

You don't look a day o - ver

COME WAKE ME UP

Words and Music by SEAN McCONNELL,
JOHAN FRANSSON, TIM LARSSON
and TOBIAS LUNDGREN

EASY

Words and Music by KATRINA ELAM
and MICHAEL MOBLEY

HERE COMES GOODBYE

Words and Music by CHRIS SLIGH
and CLINT LAGERBERG

Moderately, in 2

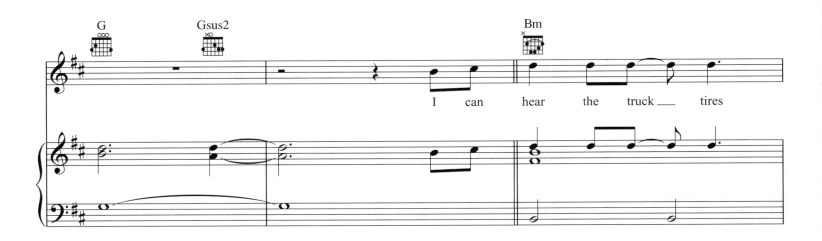

I can hear the truck___ tires

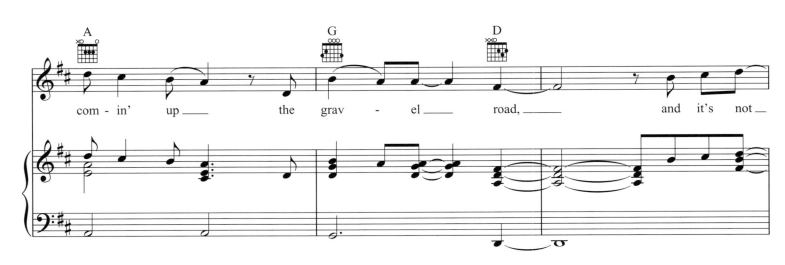

com-in' up ___ the grav - el ___ road, ___ and it's not ___

Here comes good - bye. _____

dim.

mp

I LIKE THE SOUND OF THAT

Words and Music by JESSE FRASURE,
SHAY MOONEY and MEGHAN TRAINOR

I love hear-in' that show-er turn on, ____ bet there's noth-in' but a towel on, on you. ____
Love the sound of the thun-der roll-in'. ____ Makes you move a lit-tle clos-er to me. ____

I MELT

Words and Music by GARY LEVOX,
WENDELL MOBLEY and NEIL THRASHER

52

look at me that way,   I   melt, _____

melt. _____

I WON'T LET GO

Words and Music by JASON SELLERS
and STEVE ROBSON

Slow Gospel Ballad

I'M MOVIN' ON

Words and Music by PHILLIP WHITE
and D. VINCENT WILLIAMS

LIFE IS A HIGHWAY

Words and Music by
TOM COCHRANE

Life's like a road _ that you trav-el on when there's one _ day here _ and the next _ day gone. _ Some-times _
all these cit-ies and all these towns, it's in my blood _ and it's all _ a-round. _ I love _

MY WISH

Words and Music by STEVE ROBSON
and JEFFREY STEELE

I hope the days come eas - y and the mo-ments pass slow and each road leads you where you want to go. And if you're

you.

May all ___

___ your dreams stay big.

Repeat and Fade

Optional Ending

MAYBERRY

Words and Music by
ARLOS DARRELL SMITH

Sometimes __ it feels __ like this __ world's _____ spin-ning __ fast-er
Sometimes __ I can hear this __ old _____ earth _____ shout-in'

than it did in the old days. ____
through the trees as the wind blows. ____

Recorded a half step higher.

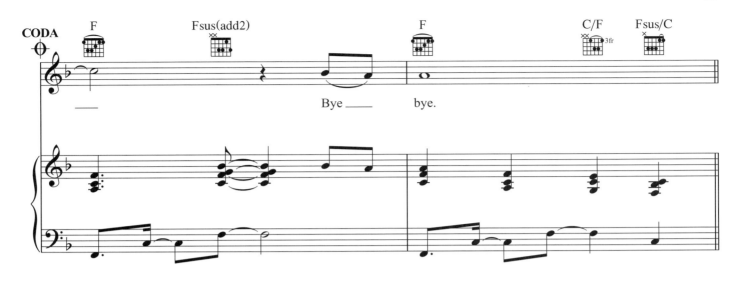

Bye ___ bye.

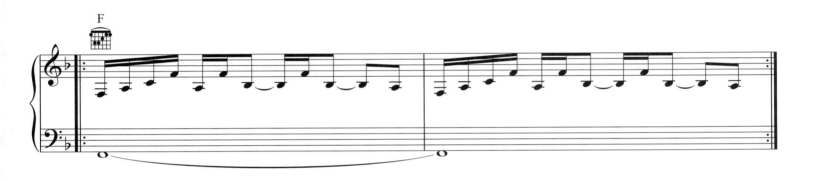

PRAYIN' FOR DAYLIGHT

Words and Music by RICK GILES
and STEVE BOGARD

Moderately fast

I _____ don't wan-na spend an-oth-er lone-ly night, ooh. _____

I've got the lights _____ turned up, the door _____ is locked, _____ the bed
I made a bad _____ mis-cal-cu-la-tion, _____ bet-tin' you _____

90

REWIND

Words and Music by CHRIS DESTEFANO,
ERIC PASLAY and ASHLEY GORLEY

STAND

Words and Music by BLAIR DALY
and DANNY ORTON

SKIN
(Sarabeth)

Words and Music by JOE HENRY
and DOUGLAS JOHNSON

SUMMER NIGHTS

Words and Music by GARY LEVOX,
BRETT JAMES and busbee

Hol - ler if you're read - y for some sum - mer _ nights. _____

Sum - mer _ nights. _

TAKE ME THERE

Words and Music by KENNY CHESNEY,
WENDELL MOBLEY and NEIL THRASHER

WHAT HURTS THE MOST

Words and Music by STEVE ROBSON
and JEFFREY STEELE

It's hard to take the rain on the roof of this emp-ty house, ___
It's hard to deal ___ with the pain of los-in' you ev-'ry - where I go, ___

to do, _____ oh. _____

WHY

Words and Music by ROBERT MATHES
and ALLEN SHAMBLIN

133